WHERE THE PARTY NEVER ENDED

GHOSTS OF THE OLD BARABOO INN

AMELIA COTTER

Other Titles by Amelia Cotter:

This House: The True Story of a Girl and a Ghost

Maryland Ghosts: Paranormal Encounters in the Free State

Breakfast with Bigfoot (ages 3-6)

First Edition:
First printing

Front cover photo and art:
Old Baraboo Inn, Copyright © 2021 by Mike Ricksecker

Back cover photo:
Old Baraboo Inn, Copyright © 2021 by Jonathan Montgomery Pollock

Poem "a wolf tree's" Copyright © 2021 by Amelia Cotter

1. Paranormal. 2. Ghosts—Wisconsin. 3. Haunted places—Wisconsin.
4. Regional/travel—Wisconsin. 5. Wisconsin—History and folklore.

PUBLISHED BY HAUNTED ROAD MEDIA, LLC
www.hauntedroadmedia.com

United States of America

Praise for *Where the Party Never Ended: Ghosts of the Old Baraboo Inn*:

"Cotter separates fact from fiction in her careful examination of the history and the mysteries behind this famous Midwestern haunt. I doubted the Old Baraboo Inn's voluminous ghostly claims until I had my own unexpected and undeniable paranormal experience there. Now, even as a skeptic, I have to acknowledge that there's something compelling going on at the Old Baraboo Inn, and Cotter captures its essence in this book."

–Allison Jornlin, writer/researcher for American Ghost Walks

"A perfectly blended mix of history, mystery, and legends. Cotter has unearthed a treasure trove of creepy and unusual stories, and expertly unravels the sordid history, unsavory characters, and numerous ghost encounters that make up one of America's most haunted places."

–Chad Lewis, author of *Paranormal Wisconsin Dells and Baraboo* and coauthor of *The Wisconsin Road Guide to Haunted Locations*

Amelia Cotter:

In loving memory of Brenda Wilder Antlitz and Tim Schoon— Two of the best friends who, wherever they may haunt, are without a doubt the life of the party!

B.C. Farr and Shelly Wells:

For Cora Haskins Gibson, our beloved Grandma, who told us true ghost stories and wrote for the Sauk County Historical Society

Curtis Farr, our beloved father, owned the Longbranch Tavern, formerly the Effinger Hotel. Sylvia Farr (nee Gibson), our beloved mother, had her first job as a waitress at the Old Baraboo Inn when it was known as Pierce's Café. This building is where they met, and the rest is history!

a wolf tree's

twisting branches—

choosing joy

ACKNOWLEDGMENTS

I would like to gratefully acknowledge the many wonderful people who contributed their expertise, feedback, photography, and stories to this book, including: Jon Cabrera, Dennis Catencamp, Thomas Dyar, Perry Foster, Alan and Judy Gould, Michael J. Heath, Dawn Holfield, Melinda Hollis, Allison Jornlin, Judy Kerl, Rachel Laverty, Chad Lewis, Kathleen Little, Jason Marten, Tammy Newkirk, Lisa Ravenelli, Michael Reagan, Ron Staton, Ronna Trapanese, and Deadgar Winter of *Deadgar's Dark Coffin Classics,* along with Debbie and Tom, Samantha, and many others. Of course, this book would not have been possible without the support of B.C. Farr, Shelly Wells, and my publisher, Mike Ricksecker at Haunted Road Media. I felt tremendous pressure to make sure that B.C. and Shelly were happy with the finished work, and that it does justice to the history, legacy, and spirits of the Old Baraboo Inn. Because of the COVID-19 pandemic, all research for this book took place from the comfort of my kitchen table home office in Chicago. To that end, I would also like to thank Gwen Herrewig, coauthor of *Haunted Baraboo,* whose detective work, guidance, and inspiration were indispensable. Finally, I would especially like to thank my husband Jonathan Montgomery Pollock for lending his photography and proofreading skills, along with countless hours of moral support, to the project. This has been an extraordinary adventure. Thank you all!

TABLE OF CONTENTS

FOREWORD

by Shelly Wells

"Sheriff! The outlaws are here!" yells the leading saloon girl, Mary, known to be the most popular of all of the ladies in Baraboo's brothel business.

"What you boys doing here?" demands the Sheriff.

"Coming for you, Sheriff," taunts the taller gunfighter, his shorter sidekick in tow.

The Sheriff glares at them, slowly moving toward them. He issues the warning: "Listen, I'm going to give you boys one chance to ride on outta' here. Now turn around and make tracks, or else you're going to meet your maker."

"You don't scare us," replies the taller gunfighter, as he and his companion move to the far end of the bar. The gamblers, girls, and whiskey-drinking cowboys hustle to get out of their way.

"Two against one, huh? Doesn't seem fair, does it, boys?" the Sheriff asks. "Keep those guns pointed at the floor, now. First one to draw is the first one to die."

Moments later… Bang, bang!

The crowd of onlookers gasp and shout. Mary rushes over to the far end of the bar, to the two bodies lying on the floor in a pool of blood. "Sheriff!" she cries. "They didn't even get a shot off!"

TIMELINE

1838	Baraboo is settled by white Europeans
1846	Baraboo becomes the county seat of Sauk County
1848	Wisconsin becomes a state; attempts ensue to forcibly remove local Native Americans from their lands
1859	George and Anna Bender open the first saloon in Baraboo on Fourth Street
1864	The structure that will come to be known as the Old Baraboo Inn is established
1866	Baraboo is incorporated as a village
1868	George and Anna Bender open the Miller-Bender Brewery
1874	George Bender dies; Anna and son Robert continue ownership of the Bender Brewery
1876 or 1879	Anna and Robert open the Bender House
1879	Baraboo welcomes a deluxe Chicago and Northwestern Railroad train depot
1882	Baraboo is incorporated as a city
1884	The Bender Brewery is destroyed by a fire; a small, unrelated fire occurs in the Bender House
1884-1918	Baraboo is hometown and Winter Quarters of the Ringling Bros. and Barnum & Bailey Circus

1885-1966	Ferdinand Effinger opens the Effinger Baraboo City Brewery, which operates under various names for the next 80 years
1890-1904	The Bender's son Frank manages the Bender House and Saloon
1905	The front corner entrance to the building is installed
1908-1917	The Bender House restaurant operates as the August Reineke Saloon until Baraboo becomes a dry city in 1917
1920-1933	The Prohibition era, a nationwide constitutional ban on the production, importation, transportation, and sale of alcoholic beverages
1921	August Reineke transfers restaurant ownership to the Bender's sons Arthur and Leroy
1929	A district judge orders the restaurant doors to be padlocked for one year after a raid on the property
1939	Pierce's Café opens in the building
1959	Circus World Museum opens
1962	John and Rose Dombroski purchase the Bender House property
1964	The Dombroski's change the name from Strikeout Club to Old Baraboo Inn
1979	John Dombroski dies; the Dombroski's son Jack purchases the business from Rose
1989	A devastating fire partially destroys the Old Baraboo Inn
1998	B.C. Farr purchases the building and renovations begin
2002	The Old Baraboo Inn reopens

INTRODUCTION

Welcome to the Old Baraboo Inn

The Old Baraboo Inn is a very cool place. In fact, the whole town of Baraboo has a real magic to it, along with a great whiskey distillery and beautiful wineries, too. In December 2018, I was invited to speak at an event at the Inn called, "The Reveal, Hunt & Celebration: World's Largest Ghost Hunt." My husband Jonathan and I were warmly greeted by the Inn's owner, B.C. Farr, and his sister, Shelly Wells, who also the volunteers with the Inn's public and paranormal events. We live in Chicago and our visit marked our first time learning about the storied histories of the town and the Inn. We were immediately drawn to Baraboo and felt welcomed at the Inn by both its living and non-living inhabitants.

The Old Baraboo Inn is an historic landmark in Baraboo, Wisconsin, and one of the Midwest's most haunted places. Operating as a bar and event venue where people can participate in a variety of historical and paranormal events, investigations, tours, and workshops, the Inn has hosted a number of local and high-profile paranormal celebrity guests and researchers, such as Brian J. Cano, Allison Jornlin, Chad

Lewis, Mary Marshall, Scotty Rorek, Shelley Mordini, and Deadgar Winter of *Deadgar's Dark Coffin Classics,* along with the Food Network and Travel Channel.

The Old Baraboo Inn today. *Photo courtesy of Michael J. Heath.*

In 2017, Food Network voted the Inn one of the ten most haunted restaurants in the country, and for good reason. One of the most remarkable aspects of the Inn's hauntings, which sets it apart from other haunted places in Baraboo and elsewhere, is the sheer volume of activity. As many as 30 spirits may haunt the Inn, and the hauntings are distinguished by intelligent, thoughtful interactions with their surroundings, as well as the movement of objects on their own. These include large, heavy objects, such as light fixtures that crash from the ceiling and barstools that fall over, stack, or turn around by themselves (sometimes with people still sitting on them!). Smaller objects also frequently move on their own and with force, such as dishes flying off their racks, photos flying off the wall, and partially deflated helium balloons seemingly picking themselves up off the floor and "chasing" people through the bar. Full body apparitions are regularly seen with the naked eye as well as photographed. Solid orblike balls of light or static are often encountered floating or shooting through the air, sometimes making physical contact with the people in their paths. Spirit voices are heard almost nightly with the naked ear as well as captured on a variety of recording devices.

B.C. notes that there are structural reasons why the building itself may be a prime conductor for paranormal activity, and why it acts as a "portal or force field" for spirits to pass through and interact with the present, physical world. Notably, the building has distinctive and memorable architecture, reminiscent of the French colonial style that calls to mind the architecture of another great haunted city, New Orleans. The proximity of the building to the nearby Baraboo River and the rock from the hillside that the Inn is built into may provide natural reinforcement for intensified spiritual energy.

In 2019, the Inn, B.C. and Shelly, Jonathan and I, and several of the people who have contributed their stories to this book, were all featured on an episode of Travel Channel's *Hometown Horror* about the town of Baraboo. The episode is delightfully named, "Three-Ring Terror"—an homage to Baraboo's infamous history as the "Circus City." After filming our segment in Baraboo in May, Jonathan and I drove up to Baraboo again in December to attend the episode's watch party at the Inn.

We teamed up with Travel Channel and Discovery+ again in 2020 for a socially distanced episode of *Fright Club*, aptly titled "Ghosts Gone Wild," with Jack Osbourne and *Ghost Brothers* stars Dalen Spratt, Juwan Mass, and Marcus

Harvey. During the Zoom interview segment, two very distinctive shadows passed along the wall behind B.C. as he sat in the front bar area with his back to the wall, alone at his laptop, to the shock and amazement of the entire *Fright Club* crew. Jack was reported to have said to one of the show's producers later, "I've been waiting for that [to happen] the whole show!"

I love the vibrant Baraboo area, as well as the friendly people and lively, playful spirits of the Old Baraboo Inn. The Inn feels like a safe-haven or stopover for a close-knit "family" of many spirits, restless and otherwise, as it has been to the living people who have passed through its doors. It has been an honor to become part of that family, and to compile this book of haunted history, ghost stories, and firsthand paranormal accounts at the Inn, in partnership with B.C. and Shelly.

B.C. Farr, owner of the Old Baraboo Inn. *Photo courtesy of the Old Baraboo Inn.*

CHAPTER 1

A Brief History of Baraboo

Baraboo is located in Sauk County, central Wisconsin, just north of Devil's Lake and just south of the popular Midwest tourist destination Wisconsin Dells. Wisconsin is densely rich with Native American mounds, history, and lore. There are more Native American burial mounds in Wisconsin than in any other state. The land that Baraboo currently occupies belonged primarily to the Ho-Chunk (previously called Winnebago) and Kickapoo Nations, and their predecessors, for centuries before being established as a settlement and trading post by white Europeans around 1838.

Paleoamericans occupied the area as many as 11,000 years ago. When white Europeans arrived in Baraboo in the 1830s, there were two established Ho-Chunk villages, one on each side of the Baraboo River. A council house and many impressive conical burial and effigy mounds were located on the grounds of what is today across the road from Circus World Museum. Baraboo was subsequently built over dozens of other conical and effigy mounds, which gradually disappeared in the ensuing decades. By the time Wisconsin became a state in 1848, many of the Indigenous People in and around Baraboo had been forced from the area onto reservations north and west of Baraboo. But many also resisted and fought back, hid, or returned later, and today the Ho-Chunk maintain a strong presence in the community. They operate multiple Ho-Chunk Gaming casinos in the region, their name is displayed on a water tower near Wisconsin Dells, and the Baraboo school mascot is the Thunderbirds. The high school periodically flies the Ho-Chunk flag on the same pole as the American flag, for the Thunderbird Day of Unity and other important occasions.

The town of Baraboo is named after the nearby Baraboo River. From there, the origin of the name itself is hotly debated, but is generally believed to be a corrupted spelling of the French surname Baribault, Baribeau, Barbeau, Rabault, or any one of a dozen or so other similar names given to the town and river on maps and in newspaper articles and personal letters during the 19th century. It seems the earliest known use of the spelling "Baraboo" was from a Wisconsin territory map in 1844.

As a municipality, Baraboo grew rapidly thanks to its ideal location along the Baraboo River and its general proximity to the Wisconsin River. Baraboo became home to flourishing flour and lumber industries, as well as a multitude of German breweries. These breweries are now gone, but their legacy can still be experienced today in the rich variety of regional craft beers and popular brand names that we associate with the Wisconsin brewing industry. Baraboo was named county seat of Sauk County in 1846, was incorporated as a village in 1866, and was incorporated as a city in 1882.

Circus animals pass in front of the Old Baraboo Inn heading south on Walnut Street, ca. 1912. *This photo has been reprinted with permission.*

The town is most well-known today for being the hometown and former Winter Quarters of the Ringling Bros. and Barnum & Bailey Circus, from 1884 through 1918 (Ringling Bros. purchased Barnum & Bailey in 1907). Baraboo was also home to several other notable circus acts in the late 19th and early 20th centuries, earning it the moniker, "Circus City." These included the Ringling brothers' first cousins' Gollmar Bros. Greatest of American Shows (1891-1916), Adam Forepaugh and Sells Bros. Enormous United Shows (1910-1911), and Wilbur W. Deppe's Classic Country Circus (1961-1966), among others. The historic AL. Ringling Theatre remains in operation, and visitors can tour the opulent AL. Ringling mansion, stop by the International Clown Hall of Fame, and view the "main attraction" at the living history site of the Circus' original Winter Quarters, the impressive Circus World Museum.

Quaint and friendly downtown Baraboo boasts bustling diners, restaurants, and storefronts that give visitors the nostalgic and romantic feeling of being suspended in time. Baraboo is also home to Man Mound, the last known surviving anthropomorphic effigy mound in North America, as well as Devil's Lake State Park, the shack and farm of legendary naturalist Aldo Leopold, and the International Crane Foundation, a sanctuary that is home to all 15 of the world's crane species, promoting and supporting crane conservation.

CHAPTER 2

The History of the Old Baraboo Inn

The Old Baraboo Inn is located at 135 Walnut Street, on the Southside Commercial District along the Baraboo riverfront, and today operates as a bar and event venue, with two apartments for rent in the upstairs half of the building. The Inn is an historic landmark that, in its relatively brief 150-year history, has been home to more than one saloon, restaurant, hotel, brewery, boarding house, billiard hall, and bar. It has long been speculated to have once been a brothel, gambling house, and Prohibition-era speakeasy[1] as well.

Perhaps due to its proximity to surrounding breweries, a train depot, and train tracks, rumors have persisted for decades that the site was once host to cowboys, flappers,

---

[1] An illicit and highly secretive establishment or part of an establishment that sold alcohol during Prohibition. The name is derived from the need for patrons requesting alcohol to keep their voices down and speak "easy."

gamblers, gangsters, and prostitutes, all looking to have a good time.

Circus elephants pass in front of the Old Baraboo Inn heading east on Lynn Street, ca. 1908. *This photo has been reprinted with permission.*

There appears to have been a dark side to all this partying, with claims of Prohibition-era (1920-1933) organized crime, frontier-style shoot-outs, forced abortions, deaths by violence, and even sexual assault. Bullet holes are visible on the façade of the building facing Walnut Street, as well as in the front bar area where, during renovations, B.C. found bullets still lodged in the holes, and on a wooden support beam in the center of the basement.

Stories abound of sites around Baraboo, including the Inn, that may have served as speakeasies during Prohibition. Allegedly, an old speakeasy was uncovered by accident in the 1930s while workers were dynamiting an ice jam in the Baraboo River near the old Ruhland Farm (close to the current location of Baraboo's wastewater treatment plant). Earlier, in 1920, two men were discovered to have been making five gallons of moonshine a day on that farm, and one of the men was shot to death by police during a standoff. Multiple other locations in and around Baraboo are now thought to have been sites where liquor was manufactured or transported during the late 1920s and early 1930s, and likely sold out the back door.

Likewise, there are a few confirmed sightings of Prohibition-era gangsters around Baraboo, with Baby Face Nelson and Tommy Carroll having been spotted in nearby Arlington and Portage. Post-Prohibition, infamous bank robber John Dillinger attended a Mass at St. Mary's Ringling Hospital shortly before his death in 1934. The Sisters did not recognize him until they saw his "Wanted" photos in the newspaper the next day.

Stories of the Old Baraboo Inn's spottily scandalous and sordid history abound, but most people agree that regardless of any indiscretions that may or may not have taken place there, the atmosphere has always remained warm, welcoming, and full of music, dancing, laughter, and *ghosts*. One can sense this immediately and palpably upon passing through the Inn's front door.

At least one private residence, owned by one Mrs. Brandenburg, stood on the lots that the Old Baraboo Inn currently occupies between the 1830s and 1860s on the northeast corner of South Bridge and Linn Street, on what is today the northeast corner of Walnut and Lynn Street. This is according to an 1885 Sanborn Fire Insurance Map and other historical records. She sold her home to the Benders in the mid-1860s and moved her six children to the north side of the river to escape the fate of having to live between two breweries. The area in Baraboo south of the Baraboo River was known as the seedier part of town, where breweries and saloons were sprouting like weeds. Thirsty locals and savvy businesspeople were drawn to the area to capitalize on the

Baraboo hub of the burgeoning Wisconsin brewing industry, as well as thriving Sauk County hops industry. This ensured that the more high-minded folks in the community stuck to the other, safer side of town.

George and Anna Bender, an enterprising couple who had emigrated from Germany in 1848, were prolific brewers whose name became foundational to the Baraboo business community. The Benders had opened the very first saloon in Baraboo, the Bender's Saloon, at 101 Fourth Street in 1859 (which to this day bears an architectural resemblance to the Old Baraboo Inn) before moving their business to South Bridge Street. They built the Miller-Bender Brewery in 1868, a few lots to the east of Mrs. Brandenburg's old home, where they brewed primarily German lager-style beer. Mrs. Brandenburg's old property had been converted into the Bender's Saloon Sample Room. Across the street from the Sample Room, on the northwest corner of South Bridge and Linn Street, stood the Ruhland Baraboo Brewery.

After George Bender died in 1874, Anna continued to operate the brewery with her oldest son, Robert, and opened a two-story hotel on the site of the Sample Room. This new establishment, called the Bender House or Bender Hotel, began operating in either 1876 or 1879 at 133-135 South Bridge Street. The building accommodated a saloon on the first level and a boarding house and hotel on the second level. It served many other functions over the next several decades, including as more than one bar, brewery, billiard hall, and restaurant. This is the structure that would come to be known as the Old Baraboo Inn.

It is important to note that the cornerstone of the Old Baraboo Inn today marks its construction in 1864, with an historic sign on the front of the building also reading, "Established in 1864." This most likely derives from when the original structure was used as the Bender's Saloon Sample Room, which must have predated the opening of the Miller-Bender Brewery and was perhaps initially related to the Bender's Saloon on Fourth Street.

The cornerstone of the Old Baraboo Inn, marking the building's construction in 1864. *Photo courtesy of Michael J. Heath.*

Serendipitously, the Chicago and Northwestern Railroad also completed work on a deluxe train depot in Baraboo in 1879, located almost directly across the street, just south and west, from the Bender House and surrounding breweries. This depot funneled even more traffic to the already-thriving businesses in the area and made the Bender House an essential stopover for travelers, railroad workers, locals, and a fair share of wandering roustabouts for decades to come.

The Bender House was a beloved pillar of the community and took on the affectionate nickname, "Ma Bender's." Meanwhile, Anna and Robert entered a business partnership with fellow brewer Ferdinand Effinger around 1879, who managed the Bender Brewery (by then no longer the Miller-Bender Brewery) until it was destroyed by a fire in 1884. He built a new brewery, the Effinger Baraboo City Brewery, on the lots to the east of the old brewery. Unrelated to the fire that destroyed the brewery, a small fire also occurred in one of the upstairs rooms of the Bender House that year, causing minimal damage. Notably, the Effinger Baraboo City Brewery took on multiple variations of the name Effinger over the years and thrived for decades before closing in 1966.

Anna's other son, Frank, managed the Bender House and Saloon from 1890, presumably after her death, until his own death in 1904. It is important to note that Anna is believed to have died, of natural causes, on the property. In 1905, the front corner entrance to the building was installed, and in 1908, the August Reineke Saloon opened, operating there until 1917, when Baraboo became a dry city (several years before national Prohibition began in 1920). Sometime around 1921, the hotel component of the business ceased operations. Reineke transferred ownership of the restaurant to two of Anna's other sons, Arthur and Leroy, who managed a restaurant onsite until 1929 when, during the height of Prohibition, a district judge ordered that the front doors to the restaurant be padlocked for one year following a raid on the property. The rest of the building's operations remained open. This is the best proof we have that the Bender brothers were up to some nefarious deeds, perhaps at the very least manufacturing and selling alcohol, if not hosting a speakeasy somewhere in the underbelly of the Bender House! The Bender family relinquished all ownership of the building sometime in the 1930s.

Between the 1930s and 1962, the building underwent various renovations and was occupied by many bars and restaurants that changed hands and names quickly. These included Pierce's Café, which opened in 1939. Interestingly,

Sylvia Farr (nee Gibson), mother of the Inn's current owner B.C. Farr, had her first job as a server at Pierce's during the early 1940s, where she met B.C.'s father, Curtis Farr. Curtis was then working at the Effinger Brewery and later owned the nearby Longbranch Tavern at 201 Lynn Street, formerly the Effinger Hotel. B.C. remembers helping his dad around the tavern as a child, developing a love for the hospitality business at an early age.

A postcard of the Chicago and Northwestern Railroad train depot in Baraboo, completed in 1879. Postcard ca. 1915. *This photo has been reprinted with permission.*

John and Rose Dombroski acquired the building in 1962 and are responsible for giving the Old Baraboo Inn its current name when, in 1964, they changed it from the "Strikeout Club." They also operated Dombroski's Package Goods on the site until 1980. John Dombroski was known as an entertaining and colorful character, and he and Rose had the reputation of always making their guests feel at home. In 1979, John died of a heart attack while standing on what is now the dancefloor in the front bar area of the Inn, leaving us with what might be the weirdest cause-of-death story I've ever heard: allegedly, a bowling ball inexplicably flew through one of the front windows of the building from the outside and, while not striking him, gave him the (final) scare of his life.

After John's death, the Dombroski's son, Jack, purchased the Inn from Rose. At some point, the building was occupied by an establishment called Bombo's Pub. In 1989, the Inn closed due to a devastating fire that destroyed part of the building. Jack, who was managing the bar that night, assisted all guests in escaping to safety. The last customer out the door on that fateful evening? None other than future owner B.C. Farr.

Left, B.C. Farr points to a bullet hole on the building's exterior. Right, close-up of another exterior bullet hole. *Photo courtesy of Michael J. Heath.*

CHAPTER 3

Renovations to the Old Baraboo Inn

After the fire in 1989, the building stood empty and in serious disrepair. B.C. Farr bought the property in 1998 and, after almost four years of intense hard work and hundreds of thousands of dollars, extensively restored it, recapturing much of its original charm. The Old Baraboo Inn reopened as a bar and grille in 2002.

Renovations began on the upstairs part of the building first, which was converted into two apartments. Renovations then continued downstairs and culminated with repairs to the basement. Notably, B.C. was able to recover and restore a portrait of John Dombroski that had been blackened with soot from the fire and was in extremely poor shape. The portrait is now displayed in the living room of one of the apartments upstairs (see page 91).

B.C. also discovered an original mural of a picturesque German countryside scene on the wall along the front bar. Today, part of the mural peeks out from behind newer layers of paint and wallpaper, with plans to continue restoring it. Additionally, the front bar features the original railing located near the stage and dancefloor area.

The Old Baraboo Inn fell into serious disrepair after a devastating fire in 1989.
Photo courtesy of the Old Baraboo Inn.

When renovations first began, B.C. and his work crew took note of the strange occurrences happening throughout the building, which became more frequent as the work continued. B.C. and crewmembers would often see shadows darting quickly, out of the corner of their eyes, and often heard phantom music and the sound of glasses clinking, as well as people laughing and talking through the walls—all while knowing the rooms on the other side were empty. They also witnessed dishes and a broom fly across the kitchen, and even saw the detachable side sprayer in the main kitchen sink moving on its own. Things got more personal when their work tools began to mysteriously disappear and then reappear later. They heard furniture shuffling around, as well as a woman crying on the first floor, and witnessed chef coats swinging by themselves in the basement.

An original mural of a German countryside scene was discovered on the wall along the front bar after the fire. *Photo courtesy of Jon Cabrera.*

B.C. recalls one of the first occurrences in which he and one of his crewmembers began to come to terms with the possibility that the building was haunted:

> "[Leftover] from the [1989] fire, there were big holes cut in the floor, on the upper and main levels of the building. You could see straight through to the basement from the top apartment level. Before I would leave for the night, I would go down to the basement and turn all the lights off. The next day I would come in and the lights in the basement would be on. I just started to question myself like, 'What's going on here?'

> "I had a guy working with me, Bruce. He comes to me one night and says, 'Let's just go make sure all the lights are off, okay?' So he goes down to the basement, and I'm watching him through the hole in the floor as he's turning all the lights off. He looks up at me, and we both acknowledge they're all off.
>
> "Next day we enter the building and unbelievable…all the lights are *on*! At this point, Bruce says to me, 'Well, B.C., I think you've got a ghost!' I did not know at the time that it was that haunted yet."

B.C. was particularly disturbed after repeatedly hearing different voices calling out his name. He thought perhaps he was working too many long hours, or that someone was playing a prank on him, or that someone was attempting to break into the building. He decided to tape the doors and windows to try and see if someone was entering the building when he and his work crew weren't around. After multiple thorough searches of the building, changing the locks, and attempting to enter a room immediately after hearing odd noises emanating from it, he never uncovered any evidence that the disturbances were being caused by other living people.

After the Inn opened, B.C. did not initially want to publicize the weird events happening there because he didn't want to scare any new customers away. He was also worried people would think he was crazy or think that he was pulling some kind of publicity stunt to draw visitors to the Inn. But eventually, guests began having experiences of their own, people started talking, and B.C. came to embrace the fact that he owned a haunted restaurant. Through his loving renovations to the Inn and the return of life to the place, the spirits of the Inn came "alive" again, as colorfully and distinctively as they had during their corporeal existence.

Mediums and psychics were also drawn to the Inn and began visiting regularly. Although little concrete history is known about what took place inside the building, they were able to independently corroborate the identities, physical appearances, and stories of several different spirits haunting the Inn. This strengthened B.C.'s comfort with and confidence in the idea of owning a haunted restaurant, and he became more vocal about the growing number of his, and others', paranormal experiences there.

Today, the Inn regularly hosts events throughout the year for new and experienced paranormal investigators, as well as for the curious and thrill seekers alike, to learn more about the Inn's spirits and hauntings and provide an opportunity to connect with them firsthand.

It is important to note that B.C. takes great care in vetting the mediums, psychics, and paranormal investigators who request to conduct paranormal research at the Old Baraboo Inn. He doesn't reveal any information to them prior to their visit, other than what can be found through internet searches. He feels a strong responsibility to care for the property appropriately and respectfully for as long as he remains the owner.

Renovations to the Inn are ongoing and should continue to shed light on the history and mysteries of the Old Baraboo Inn.

CHAPTER 4

...And the Hauntings That Followed

A marquee on the front of the Inn reads in big black letters, "HOME OF THE GHOST BOMB." A sign across the inside wall of the back bar area says, "I got GHOST BOMBED at the OLD BARABOO INN." A "Ghost Bomb" is not only a shot you can order at the bar, but to *be* "Ghost Bombed" means to be overwhelmed by the paranormal activity at the Inn through a strong, emotional encounter, and to leave a believer…if one was not already.

These encounters can sometimes be quite frightening and rarely result in minor injuries, but the overwhelming sentiment is that the spirits are a lively cast of characters who may be a little gruff and rough around the edges—as they must have been in life—but are mostly playful and simply get a kick out of interacting with their human counterparts.

Melinda Hollis, a patron and participant at a ghost hunt sponsored by the Inn, explains how it feels to "get Ghost Bombed:"

> "I visited the Old Baraboo Inn and participated in a ghost hunt. Within the first 30 minutes, I captured what I think was a ghost or spirit on video. Within minutes of capturing the ghost, I suddenly felt hot, my face felt flush and turned red, even my ears felt hot! I became dizzy and had to sit down. I was brought a glass of water and it soon passed. I was told I was possibly hugged by a ghost! The experience was amazing."

B.C. Farr, his sister Shelly Wells, and the Inn's many dedicated investigators and visitors have estimated that as many as 30 spirits may haunt the Inn. Among the most frequent and frightening encounters include witnessing objects throughout the bar and kitchen areas move on their own, sightings and photographs of disembodied arms and legs moving through the front and back bar areas, and hearing the cries of a baby and a woman (or multiple women) coming from the basement.

Patrons in the front and back bar areas have witnessed bar stools tipping over or turning around by themselves, as if beckoning the onlooker to sit down in them. The front door of the Inn will periodically open and slam shut on its own. Guests will hear someone calling or whispering their name.

Guests sitting at the front bar will sometimes feel the sensation of children climbing into their laps, and the spirits of a little boy and his dog are sometimes seen or captured on film. Guests who bring their children along may find them playing in the back bar area with what are presumed to be ghost children—laughing and twirling around as if they are holding another pair of small, spectral hands. These child spirits may be echoes of the time when the Inn was believed to have served as a home and school for the children of its tenants or workers.

Possible photo of the spirits of a little boy and his dog, sometimes seen or captured on film in the front bar area. *Photo courtesy of the Old Baraboo Inn.*

Patrons in the highly active back bar area have seen and photographed a man dressed like a cowboy, known as "Jed," and a woman in a white dress, known as "Cybil," who is seen floating in the air several feet above the floor. Guests will also frequently see and photograph faces in the multiple mirrors in the back bar area.

The women's restroom is a hotspot for activity and is said to be occupied by the ghost of former owner Rose Dombroski, who demonstrates her presence through the strong odor of old-fashioned rose oil or perfume. Several mediums have claimed to speak with her, as well as with her husband, John. Apparently, John is proud of how B.C. is taking care of the place. George and Anna Bender also make their presence known from time to time, as each of their names has come through on spirit communication devices, such as digital recorders and spirit boxes.[2] These devices are designed to capture disembodied voices[3] or electronic voice phenomena (EVP[4]).

Tenants of the upstairs apartments, as well as one lucky, or perhaps unlucky, Budweiser salesman, have also seen the ghost of an old woman that B.C and Shelly believe is Anna. Mediums claim that both Anna and Rose stick around to lovingly watch over the modern-day people and operations of their beloved Inn.

---

[2] Also known as a ghost box or Frank's box, a spirit box is a device that utilizes a radio with a rapid frequency scan mode meant to detect spirit voices and words, and allow spirits to communicate in real time.

[3] A disembodied voice is a sound heard with one's own ears, which is not channeled through an electronic/recording device and is believed to be paranormal in origin.

[4] Electronic voice phenomena (EVP) are sounds captured on electronic/recording devices that are believed to be paranormal in origin.

Additional, frightening faces appear in this mirror alongside the female guest facing left. Guests frequently photograph ghostly faces in the multiple mirrors in the back bar area. *Photo courtesy of the Old Baraboo Inn.*

One controversial spirit voice captured at the Inn claims to be none other than infamous Chicagoland gangster Al Capone, who is rumored to have been an honored guest at the Inn during his lifetime. Although there is no hard evidence of him ever having visited the Inn (as with most of his haunts both during his life and after), a rumor persists that one of his descendants may be in possession of a photo of him taken there. Additionally, the same distinct, gruff voice has been heard on separate devices time and again, answering to his name. Several mediums have communicated with who they believed to be the spirit of Capone. Capone was and remains an evasive character, as his spirit allegedly haunts other locales around Chicagoland and beyond, often with little evidence to back the claims. The Inn, however, boasts consistent and impressive interactions with a spirit who could very well be the man himself.

Numerous people have also heard a spirit known as "The Whistler" whistling a happy tune throughout the Inn. Once, B.C. was even "chased" from the back bar to the front bar by a partially deflated leprechaun-shaped helium balloon after a St. Patrick's Day event. The balloon, which had been placed in a hutch and had a weight at the bottom of its string, followed B.C. through the bar and all the way around a pool table before he stabbed it with a pen. A light fixture in one of the upstairs bedrooms once came crashing down from the ceiling onto a bed without warning.

B.C., like many paranormal researchers, believes that the hauntings are primarily associated with untimely deaths. He even speaks of a "ghost train" and its lost-in-time passengers who occasionally pass through or visit the Inn, deepening the romantic conviction that the Inn is a portal of sorts through which many kinds of spirits are able and welcome to move through or make a stopover at.

There is, in fact, a local legend in Baraboo about a ghost train, although it is not tied to any one specific train accident in the area. Interestingly, the nearby Circus World Museum houses some of the wagons from the tragic Hammond Circus Train Wreck of 1918, one of the worst train wrecks in U.S. history. Of the 400 passengers, who were performers from the Hagenbeck-Wallace Circus, at least 86 people were killed and another 127 were wounded after the train collided with another train near Hammond, Indiana. The wreck was caused by a locomotive engineer who fell asleep on the job. It appears the ghost train legend thrives in Baraboo to this day, as over the years many people have heard phantom train bells ringing or seen gates lowering and lights flashing, then lifting and turning off again, with no sign of an actual train.

B.C. describes the ghost train as full of people from various time periods and planes of existence, including circus performers, cowboys, gamblers, and other forgotten faces and characters from around Baraboo and beyond—even a lonely waitress named Matilda. B.C. claims that some of the passengers from the train stop into the Inn occasionally, much as they might have in life on a stopover at the nearby train depot, on their journey between Chicago and Minneapolis.

B.C. was working in the kitchen early one Saturday morning when he looked up from the oven and saw something bright orange out of the corner of his eye. He also thought he glimpsed a pair of legs. He whipped his head around and saw a man standing in the corner of the kitchen:

> "I looked over and there was a guy standing there, a full body apparition with a blank, death-stare face. He was wearing what looked like a 'circus shirt.' It had blousy sleeves and orange stripes with ruffles. I remember just looking at this guy, and he just looked back at me. Then he slowly disappeared.
>
> "I pictured him as a juggler or riding a unicycle. He was a fairly stocky guy. Maybe he was attracted to the smell of the prime rib I was preparing. I could tell he liked it."

A shadowy arm and leg disappear into the women's restroom. An attempt to recreate and debunk the photo with a living person was unsuccessful. This photo was selected by Brian J. Cano for his traveling "History of the Paranormal Exhibit." *Photo courtesy of Tammy Newkirk.*

One of B.C.'s most memorable otherworldly experiences at the Inn happened one night shortly after closing time. After locking up for the night, B.C. and his partner at the time headed home. He suddenly became concerned that he hadn't shut all the lights off in the kitchen, so he and his partner turned around and went back. Upon reentering the building, B.C. could see that all the lights in the kitchen, and elsewhere in the building, were off. But he noticed an odd glow in the kitchen and, as he approached the swinging doors to double-check, he saw what appeared to be a swarm of small, bright balls of light orbiting each other near the kitchen ceiling. He quickly reset the alarm and got out of the building as fast as he could.

On his way home, he received a call from the Baraboo police informing him that they were en route to the Inn because the burglar alarm was going off. B.C. then turned around again and went back, this time with the police in tow. They discovered that a lamp in the bar had been turned on, but after a thorough search, the police—who themselves seemed spooked, especially by the basement—found no signs of forced entry and concluded that it was a false alarm. Of course, B.C. and his partner had other ideas about what might have caused the alarm to go off…

The next morning, they arrived early to set up for the day. While working in the kitchen, B.C.'s partner witnessed a small, flying ball of light zip past her face—twice! B.C. later learned that the alarm at the Inn had been known to go off previously in the middle of the night, yielding false alarms every time. In a fascinating connection with the greater town of Baraboo, B.C. also heard tales that sometimes *other* burglar alarms would go off around town, around the exact same time of night, also yielding false alarms.

Visitors to the Old Baraboo Inn might experience any of the above, or any one or more of the following:

The kitchen's food bell, which rings on its own at all hours. *Photo courtesy of Michael J. Heath.*

- Seeing: battery drain in cameras, flashlights, and laptops; cell phones and cameras taking pictures on their own; floating or shooting three-dimensional solid balls of light or static (referred to in this book as "orbs"); full body and partial apparitions; movement of objects; mysterious shadows and unexplained mists; objects disappearing and reappearing; objects moving on their own with force

- Hearing: a cat meow; crying, laughing, or moaning; disembodied voices calling out names or yelling, "Hello!," "Hey, honey!," and "Woohoo!;" flirtatious whistling; the kitchen's food bell ringing on its own

- Smelling: cigar smoke, formaldehyde (especially in the women's restroom), old-fashioned perfume, roses

- Feeling: extreme changes in temperature, especially around the legs; the sensation of being caressed, jabbed, poked, or touched; tingling on the back of the neck

The most common word used by guests to describe their experiences at the Inn is "weird." So, speaking of "weird," let's explore more of the Inn's four distinctive areas, each with its own unique character, hauntings, and spirits—although the spirits are not necessarily confined to these areas—and read some firsthand accounts of peoples' remarkable paranormal experiences in each of them.

CHAPTER 5

Front Bar: Old Honky-Tonk Saloon

The Inn's front bar area is affectionately referred to as the "Old Honky-Tonk Saloon" and constitutes the main bar, dining, kitchen, and stage areas.

B.C. and other guests have seen ghostly arms and legs mingling in the crowds of regular, living patrons during busy evenings at the bar. Staff and visitors have reported seeing "sparkly" orbs of light or static that fly through the bar, sometimes leading the eye in the direction of a pair of disembodied arms or legs, or the floating torso of a spirit. B.C. has spotted patrons at the bar who seem out of place, dressed in odd costumes or period clothing. Upon a second glance, they've vanished.

As mentioned previously, a Budweiser salesman once encountered the ghost of an older woman in the front bar area that B.C. and Shelly believe is Anna Bender. In 2005, he visited the Inn before opening hours to hang signs and display promotional material. He apparently spent the better part of his visit mocking the idea of the Inn being haunted, until he had a life-changing experience.

Front bar area, photographed during a costumed "living history" event at the Old Baraboo Inn. *Photo courtesy of the Old Baraboo Inn.*

He was standing behind the bar, with B.C. nearby, when he felt compelled to look to his right, toward the doorway between the front and back bars. When he did so, he saw a woman standing in the doorway, glaring at him. He shouted, "Holy shit!"

At the same time, B.C. felt a strong pulling sensation from that side of the room and looked over toward the doorway, catching a glimpse of her as she vanished into the wall. Although she only appeared for a moment, the salesman was able to provide a clear and concise physical description of her, including that her face was quite wrinkled and that she "wore a dress reminiscent of *Little House on the Prairie*." The experience left the salesman shaken and distraught, and he changed his delivery route soon after.

A couple of employees from Sysco have also had strange encounters in the front bar and kitchen areas. One representative was alone in the building with B.C. and standing in the front bar area, arranging a delivery, when she witnessed the swinging doors to the kitchen swing open and close by themselves. She brought this to B.C.'s attention, and when they entered the kitchen to investigate, they found a pile of steel pots and pans stacked neatly on top of each other on the kitchen floor. Her response to the incredible sight: "Oh my God, would you look at that. Okay."

B.C. was shocked, but this was not the first time he had witnessed activity like this in the kitchen or near the front bar area. On another occasion, he and a skeptical friend were alone by the bar when they heard items falling and breaking in the kitchen. B.C. rushed through the kitchen doors and witnessed two stacks of plates flying at an upward angle, alternating from each other, and crashing into the wall above the dishwasher. After he yelled for the activity to stop, because plates are expensive, it quieted. He then surveyed the mess and asked, "Who is going to clean this up?" A broom flew toward him from the closet and landed on the pile of broken plates.

On yet another occasion, he was the first person to arrive in the building one morning, after being the last one to leave the night before, and discovered a cluster of bar stools arranged in a "teepee" shape in the center of the bar.

A supervisor from Sysco was sitting at the bar one time and chatting with B.C., who was standing behind the bar and leaning on the counter. According to B.C., "a large orb came flying through the doorway between the back bar and the front bar, hit my elbow, and the damn thing spun me around. Boom! Like, yeah, thanks man. Takes your breath away." The supervisor witnessed the incident and was left utterly speechless as well.

On another occasion, a delivery man who had dropped off some meat in the kitchen declared that he did not believe in ghosts. Moments later he removed his hat and remarked that he felt like he had just been hit by something. Then he felt like he was hit again. As he ran out the back door, he heard a disembodied voice call after him, "Well, I'll see you, buddy!"

One of the most beloved spirits of the Inn is that of an alleged prostitute and beautiful young woman named "Mary," who is believed to have died tragically at the Inn around 1903. Two other prostitutes are also said to have died on the premises. Some mediums have reported that the sounds of a woman heard crying in the basement are Mary, who may have been assaulted or murdered down there, or both. B.C. believes Mary was sexually assaulted and later murdered or died from a botched abortion in the basement.

In fact, there are two Marys who haunt the Inn. The other Mary, known as "Miss Mary," was apparently a schoolteacher whose spirit is confined primarily to the basement. We'll encounter her again later and learn more about her story in the chapter, "The Basement."

Whatever may have happened to courtesan Mary, her spirit remains at the Inn and enjoys being the life of the party. Mary's ghostly image has been captured in the front bar area on film, and she is often seen wearing a bright red or other light-colored dress with large, bejeweled earrings and a feather in her hair. She can sometimes be seen dancing to her favorite jukebox song, "The House Is Rockin,'" by Stevie Ray Vaughn. A patron once came into the Inn and told B.C. he was there to help him with his "problem," passing him a note behind the bar with a list of women's names who he claimed had died on the property. The name "Mary" was on the list, with her year of death listed as 1903. Notably, the song's jukebox number is 19/03.

This photo of the Old Baraboo Inn's alleged prostitute ghost "Mary" made front page news in 2003 after repeatedly flying off the wall from behind the bar toward customers…especially women with blonde hair. *Photo courtesy of Michael J. Heath.*

Mary is also likely to show up in photos during costumed "living history" events at the Inn, where guests are encouraged to dress up like cowboys and saloon girls. One visitor even shared a compelling spirit photo of what looked like Mary with B.C., who displayed it behind the bar. The photo repeatedly "flew" off its nail on the wall toward customers seated at the bar, particularly women with blonde hair, until B.C. finally had to take it down. The story of the flying photo made it onto the front page of the *Baraboo News Republic* on October 31, 2003. Occasionally, a bottle of Jack Daniels will also fly off the shelf and break into a thousand pieces on the floor.

More personal accounts of the spirits and hauntings in the front bar area abound. Allison Jornlin had a strange experience a few years ago when she and her brother, Mike Huberty, were special guests at the Inn. Allison had just given a presentation in the back bar area and found herself alone in the front bar area, setting up for a live podcast session, to be followed by a musical performance by Mike. Allison was near the main bar, stowing some equipment under a table, when she stood up and glanced across the room. "I saw this 'thing,'" she explains, "about the size of a ping-pong ball, solid, and off-white to yellowish in color…floating there." It took off suddenly, zooming past Allison's ear. "There was no feeling, no sound, I just saw it. And I flinched. I was convinced of its authenticity, like when something is whipped at your head—you flinch." She looked around but lost sight of it. Allison found the experience so odd she didn't tell anyone until several days later, when she finally confided what had happened to Mike.

One year later, Allison was in the audience of a panel that Shelly was a guest on at the Milwaukee Paranormal Conference. Shelly was describing the types of extraordinary paranormal activity experienced at the Inn and happened to mention that an old girlfriend of B.C. used to complain about being "dive-bombed by orbs" whenever she would visit the Inn. This cemented in Allison's mind that her experience had been very, very real.

Dennis Catencamp, who also appeared on the "Three-Ring Terror" episode of Travel Channel's *Hometown Horror*, shares his encounters at the Inn from an event in 2015:

> "It was December 2015, and I was attending a 'Dinner with the Dead' event at the Inn. I had been to the Inn several times before but had

never experienced anything out of the ordinary. There were about eight of us, including coworkers and friends at the table.

Dennis Catencamp, pictured here at the front bar after filming the Baraboo episode of Travel Channel's *Hometown Horror*, has had paranormal encounters in several areas of the building. *Photo courtesy of Dennis Catencamp.*

"I got up to go to the bar to get drinks for the table. The bartender took my order and turned around to fill it. Suddenly, I was tapped on the head three times. I quickly looked around to see who tapped me, and no one was even near me. I looked up to see if maybe water had dripped on me, or if there was a decoration above my head. There was nothing. I could not figure out what had caused that feeling.

"I went back to the table and told my friends what had just happened to me. Later in the evening, our devices captured some unusual activity. When we reviewed our voice-activated recorder after the event, we realized we had picked up some incredible things.

"At one point, one of us at the table sneezed and a spirit voice responded, 'Bless you.'

"At another point, we picked up a little boy's voice saying, 'Please don't hurt me.' There were no little boys in attendance.

"I put a quarter on the table and my device[5] said the word, 'Quarter.' My friend Gail's device said, 'Dollar.' So, I put a dollar on the table, at which point Gail's device replied,

[5] Going by a variety of brand names, this electronic speech-synthesis device measures electromagnetic fields and uses a built-in catalog of pre-recorded syllables and words meant to emit words and short sentences that allow spirits to communicate in real time.

> "Laid." I guess that would be expected in a place with a brothel!
>
> "At the end of the night, B.C. and another presenter brought around a spirit box. Several people spoke into it and didn't get a response. When it was my turn, I asked who tapped me on the head. Immediately, a voice from the spirit box replied, 'Paula.'
>
> "That was the night that I became a true believer in the presence of spirits."

Paranormal investigators Alan and Judy Gould share their experiences from an event at the Inn in 2018:

> "We are Alan and Judy Gould from Bristol, Indiana. We have been doing paranormal investigations for the last eight years. We have a small paranormal investigation team called Positive Energy Paranormal. We are avid motorcycle riders. When we take our vacations, we manage to pack all our equipment onto our motorcycles. While on vacation, we always try and stay where we can investigate. We found the Old Baraboo Inn and called about staying there for an overnight investigation.
>
> "B.C. set us up. We rode in on July 5, 2018. We really liked the way the Inn looked. Upon arrival, B.C. took us upstairs to our room. On the way up, we felt we were not alone. B.C. felt

the same, and he said, 'They must really like you, because they do not usually come out to greet people this quickly.' We squared our bags away and went downstairs to get some dinner. B.C. asked if we wanted to bring our equipment downstairs with us.

"We brought our spirit box, K2 meter[6], and recorders, and started a session asking if anyone there had ever had a steak, because that was what we were eating. A spirit on the spirit box answered, 'Yeah.' There were so many voices coming through. We set our K2 meter on the bar when we felt someone walk in. The temperature in the room dropped and became cold. The K2 meter was lighting up deep into the red.

"Alan left the room at some point, and I asked the spirits if they knew where he had gone. The spirit box answered, 'The basement.'

"When Alan came back, I asked him where he had been, and he answered, 'The basement.' So, we decided to play a game. Alan said, 'I am going to go hide. See what they say.'

"After a few minutes, I asked, 'Where is Alan?'

---

[6] A K2 EMF meter is a consumer-electronic device that measures electromagnetic fields and radiation and is used to contact spirits by utilizing a range of colorful lights that a spirit can allegedly trigger when present.

View from the back bar area into the front bar area. *Photo courtesy of the author.*

"The spirit box answered, 'He's hiding.' Alan heard laughter, and when he came back into the front bar, the spirit box said, 'There he is.'

> "Later that evening, Alan went to go use the men's restroom, so I asked, 'Where is Alan now?' The spirit box answered, 'In the piss hole,' which is an old term for outhouse.
>
> "We would like to thank B.C. for letting us investigate the Baraboo Inn. We had a great time and would like to come back if B.C. will have us!"

Photographer and longtime patron of the Inn, Jason Marten, shares his jarring experience in which he watched a barstool flip over by itself:

> "One evening, my girlfriend Mary and I were entertaining another couple who were visiting from Minnesota. We wanted to take our friends out for a good time, so we brought them to the Old Baraboo Inn. When we arrived, the four of us bellied up to the bar. Towards the other end of the bar was another small group of people.
>
> "My girlfriend and our two friends went to use the restroom, and a few of the people at the other end of the bar also went to the restroom, except for one person, meaning there were only two of us at the bar when this incident happened.
>
> "Out of nowhere, one of the bar stools flipped on its side and made a loud crashing bang as it hit the floor. The other person who was sitting

> at the bar was closer to that stool than I was. This person was visibly shaken. We both looked at each other asking, 'Did you just see that?' There was no one else around, and I could see no cause for what had just happened. Our friends all returned, and we were excited and in disbelief about what we had just witnessed."

Another longtime patron of the Inn, Ron Staton, weighs in with a variety of encounters over the course of his many visits to the Inn, including another self-flipping bar stool:

> "My first experience at the Inn was when an orb flew in from the back bar by the pool table area into the front bar where B.C. and I were talking. The orb hit B.C. in the arm and then went into the kitchen. I couldn't believe I saw that.
>
> "The next time I was at the Inn was with my wife, Angie. We were at the bar with a couple of friends, and a barstool tipped over by itself right next to us. When we were leaving the bar through the front door, something grabbed me in the back. I thought Angie did it, but she said she hadn't touched me.
>
> "Angie also recorded an orb on her phone. It was flying around the floor and then went into a person's jacket that was hanging over a barstool.

"I have also felt like someone was rubbing my leg while I was sitting at the bar. And a few times, I have heard someone say, 'Hello' behind me, but there was never anyone there."

CHAPTER 6

Back Bar: The Gangster Bar

The Inn's back bar area goes by the moniker "The Gangster Bar," in part due to the overwhelming aroma of cigar smoke often experienced there, and is adorned with a small bar, pool tables, pinball machines, and an area walled off with wooden panels called "The Outhouse." The back bar area is thought to have been the hot spot for the Inn's Prohibition-era foray into illegal gambling and illicit alcohol sales, and also served as Dombroski's Package Goods (and liquor store) under the ownership of John and Rose Dombroski in the later 20th century.

As mentioned previously, the back bar is one the most highly active areas of the building, where much of the paranormal activity at the Inn is experienced. A couple visited the Inn one day with their young son, and the boy wandered off to do some exploring on his own. B.C. and the boy's parents heard him in the back bar area saying "Daddy" over and over, and pointing up at something in the room. One of them snapped a photo of him, and the child explained he had been walking around and talking to a "nice old man." The boy and photographer were alone in the room when the photo was taken, but when the picture was developed, it showed the boy standing in front of the shadowy form of John Dombroski. Other people have seen or photographed an unexplained mist in that area.

Partial view of the back bar area. *Photo courtesy of the author.*

Photo of a young boy with the shadowy form of John Dombroski. The boy, who wandered away from his parents during a visit to the Inn, explained that he had been walking around and talking to a "nice old man." *Photo courtesy of the Old Baraboo Inn.*

The women's restroom is located in the far corner of the back bar area, behind "The Outhouse," and as mentioned previously, is one of Rose's hangouts, but she's not alone in there. The cowboy spirit, who some mediums have identified as "Jed," apparently sometimes joins her, although his apparition is also seen in person or in photos in other parts of the back bar area. He allegedly died violently from head injuries at the bottom of the basement stairs from either a gunshot wound, or a nasty fall, or both. He can be seen wearing a brown cowboy hat and vest. Someone in the bathroom can be heard sobbing from time to time, toilets will often flush on their own, and women have reported having their clothing and zippers pulled or played with in there.

The Old Baraboo Inn's cowboy ghost "Jed" appears (with closeup) in one of the mirrors of the back bar area, where he is often seen or felt. *Photo courtesy Michael Reagan.*

B.C. recommends that women go to the restroom with a friend and not alone, and the doorway of the bathroom is deliberately propped open with a trashcan to prevent people from being locked inside. The trashcan itself will sometimes be moved or slide in front of the door to a stall while the stall is occupied. B.C. has been alone in the building when he's heard the toilet lids slamming up and down in the stalls and the toilets flushing by themselves.

Likewise, men have also reported someone pulling on their zippers, both in the men's restroom and in the back bar area. There seems to be a devious spirit who likes to touch people back there, known only as "The Groper." The men's restroom is located a little further down the hallway from the women's restroom, behind the bar and next to the kitchen. Patron Ron Staton once heard a woman's voice say, "Hey, honey," while he was doing his business in there. He asked B.C. if anyone had gone into the women's restroom at the same time, or was trying to play a joke on him, and B.C. confirmed there had been no one else around at the time.

A common sighting in the back bar area is that of the "Woman in White," known as "Cybil." She may make an occasional appearance in the front bar area as well, but most patrons have seen her in the form of a full-body apparition in the back bar area, while others may only catch a glimpse of a white dress or skirt floating around the corner of the bar. She is responsible for one of the most arresting and creepy spirit photos I have ever seen.

There are numerous other fascinating firsthand accounts of activity from the back bar area. Regular Inn patrons Debbie and Tom share their encounter with Cybil:

The Old Baraboo Inn's mysterious "Woman in White," known as "Cybil," appears (with closeup) with her back to us in one of the mirrors of the back bar area, where she is often seen or felt. In the author's opinion, this is one of the coolest and creepiest ghost photos ever captured. *Photo courtesy of Thomas Dyar, Sauk County Paranormal.*

> "Tom and I did an overnight investigation at the Old Baraboo Inn in June of 2018. Before our investigation started, we participated in a tour of the property with others. During the tour, there were a few interesting things that happened.
>
> "When we were in the [back bar's] pool table area, we were using a spirit box. We have personally never felt this tool was worth having. We have seen many groups use them and only random words are ever said that cannot really be validated. Our group was asking questions to the female spirit there, and to our surprise, we all heard a female voice on the spirit box say her name, 'Cybil!' After that, our [paranormal investigation] team went out and bought one those boxes!"

A ghostly dog has been seen and photographed in the front bar area, but Samantha, an attendee at one of the Inn's paranormal events, recalls her encounter in the back bar area with a ghostly cat:

> "I'm a strong believer in the paranormal, both in people and animal spirits. After seeing an advertisement for a ghost hunting workshop at the Old Baraboo Inn, I took the opportunity to experience my very first ghost hunt. I'm a very open-minded individual and have had some things that can't be explained happen to me before.

"On July 28, 2018, my partner and I traveled from my hometown to Baraboo, a three-hour drive. Upon arriving, I knew this adventure would turn into an exciting night. Everyone began mingling and getting to know each other, checking out the Inn, and enjoying the meal that was provided. Afterward, everyone proceeded into the back bar. My partner and I sat at the bar and watched a presentation about past ghost hunts at the Inn. I began to feel something rubbing against my leg. I brushed it off as just my capris touching the lower part of the bar. It kept happening.

"My partner looks at me asking, 'What are you doing? Why are you brushing your legs?' I told him it felt like something was rubbing against my legs. During the presentation, a little boy and his dog were mentioned. I instantly thought, 'It's got to be the dog.' About then, my thought suddenly changed. 'Not a dog…It's a cat.' The feeling happened again, but this time I could feel that it was a long, slinky body and tail. I asked if anyone had seen or heard a ghost cat at the Inn before. It was pointed out that someone had a video from up in the apartments and 'Old Brothel' area of what sounded like a cat. I let it be known that it felt like a cat was rubbing against my legs.

"Exploring the bar areas, I went into the back bar by myself. Snapped a few photos, not expecting to see anything. Later, when everyone was looking through their photos and videos, I noticed a black figure in one photo. I enlarged the area in the photo. It was a mirror. In the mirror was what appeared to be a cat stretching. Black body and tail. The tail was down with a curl at the end. I caught the mysterious cat in a photo!"

Possible photo of the spirit of a cat that guests see, hear, and feel in the back bar area. Circle in the photo added by Shelly Wells. *Photo courtesy of the Old Baraboo Inn.*

Best friends Judy Kerl and Rachel Laverty attended a St. Patrick's Day event at the Inn to celebrate Rachel's birthday, which falls on St. Patrick's Day. In addition to this being the night of the infamous leprechaun balloon, Judy recounts her life-changing experience from the evening:

> "I don't know exactly where to start, so I guess I'll start from the beginning. My best friend Rachel's birthday is on Saint Patrick's Day. We always like to do something fun and interesting to celebrate, so last year I decided to take her to the old Baraboo Inn and experience their ghost tour.
>
> "We arrived in our leprechaun apparel ready for shenanigans. Before we went into the Inn, Rachel handed me some crystals in the parking lot for both protection and bringing forth spirits. I put them in my pocket—no one else saw me do this.
>
> "When we entered the Inn, we met with a group that was fun and friendly, and there was a wonderfully positive atmosphere. We were very excited to take our turn using the spirit box that an investigator named Mike had available for us to use. The group of participants were all asking the spirits questions through the box. They were answering, too! We got replies from several spirits, including the cowboy, a little girl, and someone called 'The Whistler.'

Best friends Judy Kerl and Rachel Laverty attended a St. Patrick's Day event at the Old Baraboo Inn, at which Judy experienced a life-changing paranormal event. *Photo courtesy of Judy Kerl.*

"I asked the spirits whose birthday it was, and the reply over the box was, 'Rachel.' Not once, but three times! That just floored us. But what happened next will stay with me for the rest of my life.

> "I asked the spirits, 'What do I have in my pocket? I brought something with me.' Both Rachel and I noticed that the temperature then dropped, at least 20 degrees, right where we were standing. No one else seemed to feel it. It was almost as if a spirit came and stood next to me to figure out what I had in my pocket. The spirit box was quiet, and then suddenly, a male spirit voice answered from the box, 'Stones.'
>
> "I reached into my pocket and pulled out the crystals. We said, 'We have crystals with us for protection. Some people call them stones.' That was truly an amazing experience! And life-changing! Thank you, B.C., for a night of spirits that was legendary."

Rachel weighs in with her side of the evening's intriguing events:

> "It is tradition for my best friend Judy and I to do something together on or around my birthday on March 17. Last year she found the Old Baraboo Inn on Facebook and said we were going to the St Patrick's Day Lucky Ghost Hunt! Seriously, two of our favorite things: spirits and leprechaun shenanigans. I have family in Baraboo, too. Turns out my cousin Jeff went to school with the owner B.C.—small world, right? When I asked B.C. about the Inn and what [the hauntings] were all about, I was told a story about the staff tossing cans down a

recycling chute behind the bar and then watching them come flying back up. Okay…I'm all in at this point.

"Before we traveled from Mineral Point, Wisconsin, for our fun night, I made a run to my favorite store, Elements LLC in Platteville, to meet up with the owner Peggy Jo. I wanted to get some crystals to take with us some for protection and to draw spirits close. Peggy is a certified crystal healer, intuitive, Reiki Master, and an amazing friend and mentor. She helped me pick out what was needed for the night in sets of two, one set for Judy and one set for me. I wasn't sure what we were getting into, but I wanted to keep us safe.

"We made our way to Baraboo in our finest leprechaun-themed attire. I gave Judy her crystals to put in her pockets before going in, and mine were already tucked away nicely in my pockets. She giggled at me but complied. I told her we were covered either way. We made our way through the door, were greeted by a 'Lurch' statue—I love that guy!—and the crowd was friendly to us strangers. We signed the waivers and get our free green beer and a coke. B.C. was so kind and fun, the crowd was friendly, you could feel the positive energy in the air.

"The history of the Inn was interesting. B.C. shared a few things, then an investigator named Mike led us on the ghost hunt. The energy in this building is incredible. All the spirits liked talking to Mike, but they loved B.C.! They even said so. We got to hear from the cowboy, who would say, 'Yup,' in an accent, as well as a little girl, and 'The Whistler.'

"Judy asked Mike's spirit box whose birthday it was. A voice answered, 'Rachel,' through the box, not once but three or four times. Apparently, the answers came from both the cowboy and 'The Whistler.' When asked if they knew the year I was born, they answered correctly on their second try.

"At the time I was a little freaked out, but more intrigued. But neither one of us was prepared for what happened next. The spirits were asked by Judy, who was standing in front of me, what was in her pockets. No one else there knew what we had. There was a little static on the box, and it got ice cold quickly. Holy crap... a spirit was checking her pockets! A voice on the spirit box said, 'Stones. You have stones in your pocket.' Then, just as quickly as it had gotten cold, the temperature went back to normal again. I will never forget that as long as I live! Incredible place!

"Later, we even heard the spirit known as 'The Whistler' whistling. It was such a neat experience."

The "Lurch" statue, unofficial mascot of the Old Baraboo Inn, greets visitors to the Inn year-round. *Photo courtesy of Judy Kerl.*

CHAPTER 7

Upstairs: Old Brothel

The Inn's upstairs area is known as the "Old Brothel," as it may have served that very purpose in the past. It is comprised of two furnished and modernized apartments. One apartment is sometimes occupied by tenants, and the other serves as a two-bedroom suite for paranormal investigations and overnight stays during the Inn's ghost hunting tours and events. It is in this apartment that the restored portrait of John Dombroski hangs in the living room, and where a light fixture once crashed from the ceiling…narrowly missing an overnight guest's head.

The upstairs is believed to be haunted primarily by a highly skilled set of ladies of the night and their satisfied gentleman callers. Other encounters upstairs include the feeling of being touched, hearing babies crying, hearing female voices, and seeing more apparitions of children, as well as orbs of light and shadow people[7].

These spirits can be helpful and kind. As mentioned previously, a light fixture in one of the upstairs bedrooms once came crashing down from the ceiling onto a bed without warning, pulling wires out of the ceiling in a blaze of sparks, blowing a fuse and tripping the breakers. A guest on an overnight stay was about to climb into that bed when it happened. He felt a pressure on his chest, as if an unseen hand was holding him back, and hesitated for just a moment—long enough to miss being hit by the falling fixture. He allegedly called B.C. from the sidewalk at 1 a.m. and had to be convinced that it was still safe for him to stay overnight in the building.

B.C. describes a baffling encounter with what he calls the "big black entity," witnessed by himself and a group of paranormal investigators one night during a routine ghost hunt at the Inn:

> "We were hearing babies crying and I was walking down the hall. We had one flashlight on. I had a weird feeling all of a sudden, and when I turned around, I looked up and there was a freaking orb—close to basketball size—just hovering near the ceiling. It started coming at me, and then it stopped.

---

[7] Shadow people or shadow figures are usually described as either human-shaped or amorphous gray to black spirit forms that are often seen out of the corner of the eye. They are sometimes, but not always, associated with dark or negative energies.

"I said, 'I see you. I'm not afraid of you. What's going on? Come talk and try to communicate with us, come on. I know you hear me, come on.'

"It started growing immensely, like a great big white mist, and then it turned into a black-bodied form, kind of like a bear. I said, 'I'm not afraid of you, come on. Come on.' And it stopped like ten feet away from me, and all these people were just completely freaked out.

"I stood there looking at it for what felt like a couple of minutes and then it just slowly faded backwards, straight back into the wall. My heart was pounding and the people in the group were like, 'Let's get the hell out of here *now*.' And it felt like something wanted us gone, but like it was just kind of 'shooing' us away.

"It was just huge and so dark, darker than the darkness around it, and had a kind of a glow, like a shadow figure, but it was a real monster—just huge and black. And you could see through it.

"We weren't sure if it was Ma Bender up there with us or not. It could have been her though, and could have been Rosie [Dombroski], too."

The furthest bedroom from the doorway to the apartment designated for paranormal events is sometimes called "The New Girls Room," where it is believed the working girls new to their trade refined their skills. Dennis Catencamp shares his encounter there:

The most haunted bedroom of the upstairs area, sometimes called "The New Girls Room." Several people, including the author, Dennis Catencamp, and a guest who was rescued by a spirit from a falling light fixture, have all experienced friendly or playful paranormal activity in this room. *Photo courtesy of the author.*

> "I had the opportunity to experiment using flashlights[8]. I placed a flashlight on the bed next to some cash I was using to entice any brothel girls to come talk with me, and I filmed the session. Nobody was near the bed and nobody would have been able to touch the

---

[8] Flashlights used to communicate with spirits will be left in the "on" position, with the tops unscrewed just enough for the light to go off and on with the slightest touch. Even spirits who may never have seen a flashlight in their lifetimes can be asked to touch the object in front of them and be prompted with "Yes"/"No" questions.

> flashlight. When I asked if anybody was there, and if they could please turn the light on, the flashlight turned on. When I asked if they could turn the light off, the flashlight turned off.
>
> "I gathered up the flashlight but left the money and got ready to leave. I said, 'Any money left on the bed is yours to keep as a tip.' Later, when reviewing the video, a female voice in the room said at that very moment, 'Bless you.'"

Deadgar's Dark Coffin Classics, a local and popular campy horror television show based in Kenosha, Wisconsin, filmed an episode of their show at the Inn. The show's cast and crew were most definitely "Ghost Bombed" during their night of frights. The show's host, Deadgar Winter, tells his tales from that fateful night:

> "I'm Deadgar Winter, host of *Deadgar's Dark Coffin Classics*. I have been invited on many ghostly adventures in the past. Here is my story of what happened during a night of filming at the Old Baraboo Inn.
>
> "My cast and crew arrived at the Inn to film the show with B.C. Farr. One of my 'Deadgirls,' who has a talent for attracting spirits, noticed right away that something wasn't right about the place. She got a heavy feeling in her chest, but it later went away. We continued to set up to film our show.

Everything was going great until we moved up to the 'Old Brothel' area to film our remaining scenes.

"As my crew were doing their sound check, one of my camera guys saw a black shadow move across the wall behind us. He kind of freaked out. We noticed a sharp drop in temperature when this happened. We continued to film. The camera crew was experiencing problems with both cameras trying to autofocus, and one camera's battery instantly draining from 80% power to 5% power in a matter of seconds. We then moved into another room and noticed orbs flying around above one of my camera guys. We then proceeded to film again, and again had issues with the cameras.

"While my crew was working it out, I sat in a chair and waited, when all of sudden something forcefully tapped me on my shoulder. I shot out of the chair—everyone saw it happen. Then one of my 'Deadgirls' went into a sort of seizure, and we had to get her back downstairs because she was in bad shape.

"We then filmed the rest of our closing scene and realized that this place was for real. When we finished, we all went down to the bar area and I felt like something had drained all my energy. My crew felt the same. My 'Deadgirl' was okay, by the way.

"This is the first time we were messed with this badly while filming a show at a haunted place. The Old Baraboo Inn is truly haunted."

Deadgar Winter and the Deadgirls, of *Deadgar's Dark Coffin Classics*, were "Ghost Bombed" during a night of filming at the Old Baraboo Inn. *Photo courtesy of Deadgar Winter.*

Professional psychic medium and spiritual coach Perry Foster, who also appeared on the "Three-Ring Terror" episode of Travel Channel's *Hometown Horror*, remembers a chilling and very emotional encounter he had upstairs with a child ghost:

> "On the evening of Saturday, December 8, 2018, at around 10 p.m., I was upstairs in one of the units that used to be part of the 'Old Brothel' area. A number of personal experiences occurred. First, I was serving as medium and was communicating with numerous spirits who would share their names with me, then confirm their names through the spirit box app we were using. Many spirits were moving around and bouncing in and out of our space. My body temperature was in constant flux between having hot flashes and cold spells, along with a constant sensation of energetic movement and buzzing.
>
> "Among the spirits coming through was a little boy who would only stay for a few seconds and then leave again. This appearing and disappearing occurred several times throughout our session. He would always appear behind me. When he would appear, I felt overwhelming fear and sadness. He kept tugging at my energy, trying to get me to leave my body and follow him to the basement. He was so scared. This boy's spirit was making several attempts to call me down to the basement, but I intentionally chose not to go

because I didn't want to leave the session I was conducting upstairs. I wanted to cry for him, but I shut the emotions down as a way not to get so absorbed by this spirit's energy. I kept my attention grounded in the room we were in and proceeded with our session.

Perry Foster, pictured here in the upstairs living room during an interview for the Baraboo episode of Travel Channel's *Hometown Horror*, experienced a chilling and emotional paranormal encounter in this area with the spirit of a little boy. The restored portrait of John Dombroski can also be seen on the wall in the background. *Photo courtesy of Perry Foster.*

> "This boy, as I saw him, looked to have been around the age of eight or nine, seemed incredibly sad and needy, and was energetically very erratic. He also appeared to me as being of color, not Caucasian or European.
>
> "There was one point when I acknowledged the young boy, turned around, and held my hand out for him to grab. He brushed my hand, then disappeared again. Each time he came through, I felt the call to leave my body and go down to the basement."

Lisa Ravenelli recalls a visit she had to the Inn with her mother and her friend, Linda, where she contacted several spirits, including that of her own father:

> "The first time I went to the Old Baraboo Inn, I was a little skeptical and really did not think anything would happen. It was just a fun girl's night out that turned eventful. After a brief introduction and explanation of the building and its history, they turned on a spirit box. My friend Linda and I heard my name being called. It was my dad, who had passed away. Tearfully, I answered and spoke to my dad through the spirit box.
>
> "It was an amazing night. Upstairs, I felt my hair being pushed off my shoulder, my necklace being moved and played with, and there was a definite smell of roses or floral

> scents in the air. The overwhelming feeling of being touched was too much for me, and at one point, I had to leave the room. I felt nauseous and drained.
>
> "Even just talking downstairs in the bar afterwards, we felt someone sitting next to us and my mom was startled by someone touching her shoulder."

Finally, I had an interesting experience of my own in "The New Girls Room." Jonathan and I briefly took part in an investigation at the Inn after the event we attended on December 8, 2018. This was the same night Perry had his profound encounter with the little boy ghost and, in fact, noted mediums and researchers Mary Marshall and Scotty Rorek had similar encounters with the little boy that night as well.

Attendees were divided into small groups that would rotate through the building at set times, but Jonathan and I were told we could explore freely (and quietly) on our own since I had been a guest speaker that day—one of the perks!

We were drawn to the upstairs apartments. Many people were up there at the time, but we managed to find a quiet space in the back two bedrooms, one of which had a set of creepy bunk beds in it, and we didn't stay in there for long. The other room, which we learned was called "The New Girls Room," had a strange closet in it that is apparently a hub of activity—several people have captured what appears to be "ghost sex" through EVP and on video in that closet! B.C. shared one of these video clips on the "Ghosts Gone Wild" episode of *Fright Club*. We were taking some photos of the closet and quietly conversing about it when I felt a hand wrap around the back of my neck. It felt like a woman's hand, with a gentle but firm touch, and I had the sense that we were being told to leave.

The message felt like, "I know you must be tired, how about you head home?" Well, we *were* tired and hadn't planned to stay for the full investigation anyway, so…we took that to mean it was time to go, and we went. We wrapped up shortly after that and headed back to our hotel for the night. I am not one to argue about bedtime.

CHAPTER 8

The Basement

The basement of the Old Baraboo Inn is perhaps the building's saddest and most mysterious location. The basement is comprised of a large space that occupies the entire footprint of the building and serves as a storage area for the Inn's bar and restaurant supplies. It has dirt floors in several areas and many small rooms and corridors, at least one of which looks like it could have been finished and painted to utilize as a speakeasy. Whereas the other areas of the Inn are marked by primarily energetic, fun, "party vibes" as B.C. likes to say, and what many describe as friendly, good energy, the basement carries the bulk of the building's darker energy. The entities here are not necessarily relegated to the basement alone, however, and are sometimes experienced in other parts of the building.

Many types of cries and sobs are heard emanating from the basement, including those of a baby and a woman, or multiple women. One of these women is believed to be the beloved prostitute, Mary. The Inn's cowboy ghost, Jed, is also thought to have died at the bottom of the basement stairs.

The Old Baraboo Inn's cowboy ghost "Jed" is thought to have died at the bottom of the basement stairs. *Photo courtesy of Michael J. Heath.*

The Inn's walk-in cooler is located near the bottom of the basement stairs, and employees retrieving or stocking items will often find themselves locked inside of it, with the light turned off, even though the door does not automatically close when left open. The spirits of the basement can also be helpful, as one bartender who found himself falling backwards down the stairs while carrying some cases of beer was caught in mid-air and lifted back up to safety.

B.C. holds the door to the walk-in cooler that employees will unwittingly find themselves locked inside of...with the lights turned off. *Photo courtesy of Michael J. Heath.*

During renovations and before fully understanding or developing a relationship with the hauntings at the Inn, B.C. partially covered an area of the dirt floor with cement, after discovering what looked like old blood stains permanently soaked into the floor. He also explains that the basement was used for gambling and has multiple exits, including a secret tunnel (which is now bricked over) and another exit leading directly out to the street. The third exit is up the staircase leading to the back of the front bar area. These exits would have been used during the Inn's brewery days to move beer, kegs, and other equipment in and out of the basement and to nearby breweries. B.C. believes these exits were also used by some of the more high-profile Prohibition-era gangsters to leave in secret or flee the Inn during alcohol raids and after other illicit activities, and that spirits still utilize the tunnel today. B.C. believes the basement was an area where the darker and sadder side of life at the Inn was experienced, including forced abortions, interrogations, and murders.

There is an odd wooden pole in one area of the basement, which acts as a support beam for the structure of the building, that appears to be riddled with bullet holes at head and stomach level. The wooden beam is referred to as the "Execution Pole." Investigators, mediums, and visitors have experienced a sensation of deep sadness near the pole, as well as feelings of choking, gagging, or suffocating, and it's believed that multiple people were tied to the pole and tortured or shot at some point during the Inn's illustrious history. B.C. has been told by more than one medium that a body may be buried in the dirt floor beneath the pole, in the same area that B.C. covered with cement. The pole is also located directly under the women's restroom and is thought to be connected to some of the activity occurring there, such as the sounds of a woman sobbing.

This wooden support beam in the basement appears to be riddled with bullet holes at head and stomach level and is referred to as both the "Interrogation Pole" and the "Execution Pole." *Photo courtesy of the author.*

One of the more intriguing entities present at the Inn, who primarily occupies the basement, is the *other* Mary—

"Miss Mary"—thought to be a schoolteacher who looked after the children living at the Inn when it was the Bender House. These children are believed to have belonged to the tenants or the ladies who worked at the Bender House at the turn of the 20th century, and they attended school in the building.

Children's schoolbooks have been found in the basement, and part of the alphabet is written in child's handwriting on a step at the bottom of the basement stairs. People have captured EVP of a child reciting her "ABCs," and many visitors have heard the disembodied voices of children calling for "Mommy!" or singing "Happy Birthday."

"ABC" appears to be etched in child's handwriting on a step at the bottom of the basement stairs, where people have also captured EVP of a child reciting the alphabet. *Photo courtesy of Michael J. Heath.*

Sketch of "Miss Mary," who haunts the basement along with some of her former students, by a psychic named Ronna. *Photo courtesy of the Old Baraboo Inn.*

In 2012, mediums Dawn Holfeld and Ronna Trapanese visited the Inn and made contact with Miss Mary, who told them she died from an illness in her early 30s. Mary requested that Ronna, who is able to illustrate what spirits looked like in life, draw a picture of her. Mary told Ronna she wanted to be drawn with her hair down, because people rarely saw her that way.

The voice of Miss Mary has been captured on recordings saying, "I'll go to my room," when mediums present have tried to discuss the circumstances of her death. When asked why her spirit remains at the Inn, especially in the basement, Mary has answered, "It's here where I feel most alive."

Dennis Catencamp has had some extraordinary experiences in the basement. Here he recalls one particularly emotional incident:

"Some of my most memorable experiences have been in the basement. I have had sensations of something coming up behind me and, of course, nothing was there when I turned around.

"One time, B.C. allowed me to sit at the bottom of the basement stairs in the dark. As I sat down, I immediately had a feeling of being crushed or squeezed. It almost made me feel ill. I asked if it was okay for me to be there. Just a few seconds after, a large round orb seemed to come from my left and proceed towards me—where it briefly stopped and hovered—before resuming movement and disappearing into the wall on the right. I was pretty shaken, and felt it was personal. I was lucky enough to capture this on camera."

CHAPTER 9

Beyond the Old Baraboo Inn: Our Visit to Man Mound

As I mentioned in the introduction, I was invited to the Inn in December 2018 to speak at an event called, "The Reveal, Hunt & Celebration: World's Largest Ghost Hunt." I would be remiss not to share the harrowing, and humorous, experience that Jonathan and I had while visiting the nearby historic and sacred landmark, Man Mound. Our story was also featured on the "Three-Ring Terror" episode of Travel Channel's *Hometown Horror*.

We were excited for the opportunity to visit Baraboo and arrived in town the day before the event. We were delighted to discover that Baraboo has a real magic to it, and spent the day sightseeing, shopping, eating, and drinking our way through town. The next morning, we were expected to arrive at the Inn by 11 a.m. and decided to have a quick breakfast and stop by Man Mound Park before heading over. Man Mound Park is located approximately three miles from Baraboo, which was about a fifteen-minute trek for us on a desolate winter road. We had a highly strange and profound experience there at around 10 a.m.

Man Mound, the last surviving anthropomorphic effigy mound in North America. *This photo has been reprinted with permission.*

We are particularly fascinated by Native American burial mounds and sacred sites, and the history of their destruction and preservation throughout the Midwest. Tiny Man Mound Park was established in 1908, placed on the National Register of Historic Places in 1978, and designated a National Historic Landmark in 2016. It lies unassumingly along the side of Man Mound Road and is home to an ancient, large, man-shaped mound, the last known surviving anthropomorphic effigy mound in North America. Ironically, the road actually cuts through the mound, separating part of Man Mound's legs from the rest of his body. The park is equipped with a small parking lot and a few benches, and is surrounded by a patch of woods and farmland on all sides.

It is important to note that there really aren't any known ghost stories associated with effigy mounds, even though they and other types of "Indian burial grounds" are continuously over-dramatized and sensationalized in modern lore. Mounds are sacred sites, and their destruction and exploitation are beyond unfortunate. My feelings regarding our experience at Man Mound do not reflect, and should not sensationalize, a white fantasy of connecting with ancient Native Americans. It was merely a strange and powerful—and somewhat funny—occurrence, which seemed to originate from the woods behind the mound, and I will share the story exactly as it happened.

The area was eerily deserted and quiet that morning. I felt unwelcome immediately, but chalked it up to the park's small, strange setting. The ground was covered in a pristine foot or so of snow, and it was clear that no one else had been at the park that morning. After a moment of getting our bearings, we were able to discern the impressive shape of the mound.

The author stands next to Man Mound on the morning of December 8, 2018.
Photo courtesy of Jonathan Montgomery Pollock.

We walked around and took some photos, careful not to touch the mound itself. Taking in the moment and reflecting on the silence and solitude of the area, we suddenly heard a loud, high-pitched wailing sound coming from the patch of woods. It startled us and we decided to wrap up our little adventure. The sound continued in short "yelps" and seemed to be moving closer, so we hurried back to the car.

Our car, which was a rental, wouldn't start. We both tried everything for several minutes and felt like dumb city folk—coming up from Chicago in our cheapy rental car with no idea how to drive in a few inches of snow.

The key wouldn't even turn in the ignition, it was freezing cold out, and the Girl Scout in me noted that we didn't have any water or snacks. In the age of Googling solutions to everything, we also had no cell or data service. In fact, Jonathan's phone didn't have any signal at all.

We decided that we would have to try and flag someone down on the side of the road. Our last resort would be knocking on the door of the farmhouse across the street—but I've seen way too many horror movies and would sooner let us freeze in the parking lot, or take our chances with the entity in the woods, than demonstrate *that* kind of courage.

We heard the high-pitched wailing sound again, even louder. Jonathan, born and raised in Chicago, declared, "It's probably just a cow." I grew up in a farming county in Maryland and have hiked around many parts of the U.S., and this was not a familiar, natural animal sound to me. I joked back to Jonathan, "It's probably Bigfoot."

All joking aside, I had begun to experience a weird crawling feeling, accompanied by the sensation of static electricity tingling through my body—as if the origin of the sound was indeed supernatural. I knew that whatever this was, whether a bobcat in distress or an otherworldly being, it wanted us gone. I actually had the sense, briefly, that we were in danger, and I felt extremely isolated despite being only a few minutes from town. The overwhelming feeling that we were unwanted did not, however, jive with the fact that our car inexplicably refused to start. You would think that whatever it was would want to expedite our departure, not stall it.

In any case, while Jonathan continued troubleshooting, I took a deep breath and dragged myself to the roadside to wait for a passing car, feeling watched from the woods as I did. It is important to note that the trees were bare and the woods were not particularly thick to begin with, so anything at or near the tree line would have been visible to us, and there were no sounds of branches breaking or anything moving quickly toward us.

No cars had passed by the park yet that morning, but thankfully, after a few minutes, a car finally went by. I waved like an idiot and watched as it kept driving down the road. I'm sure the people in it were deliberating over whether or not they should stop. After about a half mile, they slowed down, turned around, and came back. By this time, the sound from the woods had subsided.

The driver, a man, got out and asked us if we needed help. We explained our embarrassing situation, and he got in our car and got it started immediately, with no trouble. A woman in the front seat also got out and, seeing how distressed we were, exclaimed, "You're so lucky—my husband owns a car dealership!" She gave each of us a big hug. There was another lady in the backseat laughing, and suddenly all was well and normal again, and it felt serendipitous that they would pass us right when we needed the kind of help they could provide (hugs included).

The man explained something about cars having trouble starting when it's cold outside, and I couldn't tell if that was his way of comforting us while secretly laughing at us, but we waved goodbye to him and his family, and away they drove.

We took a minute to gather ourselves and get settled back in the car. When we finally pulled out of the parking lot, I felt and heard a loud smack on the rear passenger window behind me. It was so human, so mundane and ordinary, that I thought it was a person. For a moment, I thought it might be the man who had just helped us knocking on the window, even though I knew we had just seen him and his family drive away. Of course, when I turned to see who it was, there was nobody there. Just the mound behind us.

I had the distinct feeling that we were being teased, that whatever we had just encountered around the mound intended only to scare us and not to hurt us, and was playfully seeing us off now that everything was okay. I felt we had just participated in a synchronistic event, and the feeling was both chilling and comforting at the same time.

When we arrived at the Inn and met everyone there for the first time, I felt compelled to share this story with everyone. I'm a professional storyteller who specializes in supernatural tales, but I don't always feel comfortable talking about my own experiences, and I definitely wouldn't share something embarrassing like how some out-of-towners got stranded in a park because our Hyundai Accent wouldn't start. But I did tell this story at the Inn that day, and the responses were not only empathetic, but many people echoed it with strange, local tales of their own about odd sounds coming from the woods around Baraboo, eerie occurrences in the liminal areas between the farmlands and forests, and even sightings of Bigfoot-like beings.

I came away relieved that I had told the story and had made so many personal connections because of it. I also felt, from that moment, a strong connection with the Old Baraboo Inn, with Man Mound, the town of Baraboo, and with all the beings we encountered there.

On our way to the car that night, after participating in the evening's investigation, as told in the "Upstairs: Old Brothel" chapter, I also found a penny in the parking lot next to my passenger door. We had learned earlier in the day that the "secret word" from the "2018 World's Largest Ghost Hunt," an event sponsored by the same people who had planned this event, was "penny." This was a word that had been written on a piece of paper and sealed in an envelope on the back of a painting. Investigators around the world were not told what it was, but were prompted to encourage spirits to "find" it and share it with them as a means of non-subliminal communication. No spirits had correctly guessed the word "penny," although they had apparently guessed the word the previous year, but many voices were captured that referred to the painting itself. The word was shared with everyone for the first time at the event we attended that day.

I have kept that penny as a reminder of our first, and certainly not last, adventure in Baraboo.

AFTERWORD

You're Cordially Invited

The Old Baraboo Inn is a friendly, fun, and historic haunted location that feels like a place suspended in time, hearkening back to multiple iconic eras in American history. The Inn is steeped in rich folklore, shrouded in myth and a profound paranormal energy, and surrounded by the fascinating history and legends of the greater Baraboo area. It's a place where many came to party and perhaps a few met their untimely end, and is a place where it seems the party never ended.

Stop by the Old Baraboo Inn for a special event, investigation, or a round of strong drinks, and get "Ghost Bombed" in the company of some truly kind people. The upstairs haunted suite is available to rent for individuals and small groups. A visit to the Inn doesn't require any special ghost hunting equipment—only an open heart and mind, and a healthy dose of respect for the phenomena that cause us all to marvel and wonder at the possibilities of life beyond death.

Plan your adventure to the Old Baraboo Inn by visiting their Facebook and YouTube pages at:

https://www.facebook.com/Old-Baraboo-Inn-119252121500427/

https://www.youtube.com/channel/UCYWS1AiePDK2YFOmONDyL-Q

That's a wrap! Friends of the Old Baraboo Inn and members of Travel Channel's film crew celebrate after filming the Baraboo episode of *Hometown Horror*. *Photo courtesy of Shelly Wells.*

Explore more of the Old Baraboo Inn by watching:

"Ghosts Gone Wild." *Fright Club,* season 1, episode 7, Discovery+, 9 Mar. 2021. *Discovery+,* https://www.discoveryplus.com/show/fright-club?fbclid=IwAR11fpBMWlyOqsE5kO3oEdCDJ6FPlSCgaVslSkiQpeFqQZ00WexZIeJIKNY.

"The Old Baraboo Inn." *Shadow Hunters,* season 1, episode 1, PARAFlixx, 5 Apr. 2021. *PARAFlixx,* https://paraflixx.vhx.tv/shadow-hunters-paraflixx-paranormal-plus/season:1/videos/paraflixx-episode-1-old-baraboo-inn-paranormal-plus.

Team OBI: An Investigation into the Haunting of the Old Baraboo Inn. Directed by Ben Wydeven, Makeshift Media Group, 2016. *Amazon Prime Video,* https://www.amazon.com/Team-OBI-Investigation-Haunting-Baraboo/dp/B01MRT7MCM.

"Three-Ring Terror." *Hometown Horror,* season 1, episode 5, Travel Channel, 2 Dec. 2019. *Amazon Prime Video,* https://www.amazon.com/gp/video/detail/B07YXG45CR.

"10 Most-Haunted Restaurants in America." Food Network, 21 Oct. 2017. *YouTube,* https://www.youtube.com/watch?v=KKalTL7-6Yc.

BIBLIOGRAPHY AND FURTHER READING

"Baraboo." *Encyclopedia Britannica*. https://www.britannica.com/place/Baraboo.

"Baraboo, Wisconsin—A Brief History." *Wisconsin Historical Society*. https://www.wisconsinhistory.org/Records/Article/CS2424.

"Baraboo's Rich Circus History." *Baraboo's Big Top Parade & Circus Celebration*. https://bigtopparade.com/circus-history.

Birmingham, Robert A. and Amy L. Rosebrough. *Indian Mounds of Wisconsin*. 2nd ed., University of Wisconsin Press, 2017.

City of Baraboo, Wisconsin. City of Baraboo Wisconsin. https://www.cityofbaraboo.com.

Daley, Jason. "Get to Know Man Mound, One of 10 New National Historic Landmarks." *Smithsonian*, 11 Nov. 2016, https://www.smithsonianmag.com/smart-news/get-to-know-man-mound-one-10-new-national-historical-landmarks-180961062.

Damask, Kevin. "Exploring haunted history: Local area full of ghoulish tales." *Juneau County Star-Times*, 11 Oct. 2016, https://www.wiscnews.com/juneaucountystartimes/ news/local/exploring-haunted-history-local-area-full-of-ghoulish-tales/article_0b7cb582-1089-5aee-b450-3a3cc256f4d8.html.

De Laruelle, Scott. "Investigators checking out reputed haunting." *La Crosse Tribune*, 21 Jun. 2005, https://lacrossetribune.com/news/investigators-checking-out-reputed-haunting/article_0e606d93-2ed1-5c49-b004-0b960c3e4ae4.html.

Erickson, Doug. "The Ghost of the Old Baraboo Inn." *Wisconsin State Journal*, 5 Jul. 2005, https://madison.com/ news/the-ghost-of-the-old-baraboo-inn-many-years-ago/article_04cfd88f-4e99-5363-ab8a-3b3284ff0d2e.html.

Herrewig, Gwen and Shelley Mordini. *Haunted Baraboo*. The History Press, 2021.

Historic Markers [City of Baraboo, Sauk County, Wisconsin]: 1982 Centennial Committee. Perry Printing, 1982.

The History of Sauk County, Wisconsin. Western Historical Company, 1880.

International Crane Foundation. International Crane Foundation. https://www.savingcranes.org.

Lamoreaux, Kim. "Plenty of 'boo's' at Old Baraboo Inn." *The Sauk Prairie Eagle*, 30 Oct. 2014, https://www.wiscnews.com/saukprairieeagle/news/local/plenty-of-boo-s-at-old-baraboo-inn/article_e3fe0c7d-e1cd-57b0-ad9e-5f5a7bd059fe.html.

Lange, Kenneth I. and Ralph T. Tuttle. *A Lake Where Spirits Live: A Human History of the Midwest's Most Popular Park.* 1975.

Lewis, Chad. *Paranormal Wisconsin Dells and Baraboo*. On the Road Publications, 2018.

Olson, Keri J. *Healing Presence, A History of Caring.* Ballindalloch Press, 2012.

"Sanborn Fire Insurance Map from Baraboo, Sauk County, Wisconsin." *Sanborn Map Company*, 4 Oct. 1885. Retrieved from Library of Congress, Geography and Map Division. https://www.loc.gov/resource/g4124bm.g094901885.

"Seize Liquor Near Baraboo." *Baraboo Weekly News*, 23 Sep. 1920.

Sauk County Historical Society. Sauk County Historical Society. https://www.saukcountyhistory.org.

Ward, Joseph. "Lynn Avenue and Lynn Street." *Baraboo 1850-2010: Chronology of the Growth of the Commercial & Retail Districts – Volume 3,* 2013. https://www.baraboopubliclibrary.org/files/local/wardvol3/06%20%20Lynn%20Avenue%20and%20Lynn%20Street.pdf.

Ward, Joseph. "Origin of the Name 'Baraboo.'" *Baraboo 1850-2010: Chronology of the Growth of the Commercial & Retail Districts – Volume 1,* 2013. https://www.baraboopubliclibrary.org/files/local/wardvol1/10%20Baraboo%20-%20How%20named%20-%20About%20Section%20D.pdf.

Ward, Joseph. "Walnut Street." *Baraboo 1850-2010: Chronology of the Growth of the Commercial & Retail Districts - Volume 5,* 2013. https://www.baraboopubliclibrary.org/sites/www.baraboopubliclibrary.org/files/local/wardvol5/04%20Walnut%20Street.pdf.

NOTE FROM THE AUTHOR

A portion of royalties from the sales of this book will benefit the ongoing restoration of the Old Baraboo Inn. Thank you for supporting and helping to preserve history!

ABOUT THE AUTHOR

Amelia Cotter is an author and storyteller with a special interest in the supernatural, history, and folklore. Amelia lives and writes in Chicago but is originally from Maryland, where she earned a degree in German and History from Hood College. She has appeared on various radio and television programs, and regularly presents at conferences and events. Amelia shares her love for the *many* wonders of the world, while hopefully inspiring others to explore it, through her books, stories, poetry, and other writing. Visit her official website at www.ameliacotter.com, or write to her any time at ameliamcotter@gmail.com.

Other Haunted Road Media titles from Amelia Cotter:

Higgypop 2020 Paranormal Entertainment Awards Winner!

Nora is a lonely fifteen-year-old who dreams of more adventure than life in suburban Maryland can offer. Fascinated by the supernatural, she begins exploring an allegedly haunted abandoned house on the property where her father works. She soon finds herself tangled in the mysteries of the house as she uncovers its many secrets and meets a shy ghost called "Walter."

Other Haunted Road Media titles from Amelia Cotter:

Join author and storyteller Amelia Cotter as she presents a chilling collection of personal paranormal encounters gathered from across Maryland—in some of its most legendary haunted locations, private homes, hidden, and sometimes unexpected places. From classic haunted houses to UFO sightings and mysterious creatures, these true stories, powerfully told in the words of those who experienced them, are sure to entertain and engage paranormal enthusiasts in Maryland and beyond.

Made in the USA
Coppell, TX
05 May 2021

55071100R00075